Money Smarts

Earning Money

by Nadia Higgins

bake sale
75¢

Bullfrog
Books

Ideas for Parents and Teachers

Bullfrog Books let children practice reading informational text at the earliest reading levels. Repetition, familiar words, and photo labels support early readers.

Before Reading

- Discuss the cover photo. What does it tell them?

- Look at the picture glossary together. Read and discuss the words.

Read the Book

- "Walk" through the book and look at the photos. Let the child ask questions. Point out the photo labels.

- Read the book to the child, or have him or her read independently.

After Reading

- Prompt the child to think more. Ask: Have you earned money? What did it teach you?

Bullfrog Books are published by Jump!
5357 Penn Avenue South
Minneapolis, MN 55419
www.jumplibrary.com

Library of Congress Cataloging-in-Publication Data is available at www.loc.gov or upon request from the publisher.

ISBN: 978-1-62031-890-4 (hardcover)
ISBN: 978-1-62031-891-1 (paperback)
ISBN: 978-1-62496-673-6 (ebook)

Editor: Jenna Trnka
Book Designer: Molly Ballanger
Photo Researcher: Molly Ballanger

Photo Credits: S _ Photo/Shutterstock, cover (bottom); Hortimages/Shutterstock, cover (left); icemani/Shutterstock, cover (right); Eme Medioli/Shutterstock, 1; WilleeCole Photography/Shutterstock, 3; ESB Professional/Shutterstock, 4; polya _ olya/Shutterstock, 5; Lucky Business/Shutterstock, 6, 23bl; dobok/iStock, 7; skynesher/iStock, 8–9; Monkey Business Images/Shutterstock, 10–11; Andrey _ Popov/Shutterstock, 11, 23tr; Caiaimage/Paul Bradbury/Getty, 12–13, 23br; Elena Hramova/Shutterstock, 14–15; Malachy666/Shutterstock, 16 (background), 23tl; Anastasia Bobrova/Shutterstock, 16 (foreground), 23tl; LWA/Dann Tarif/Getty, 17; Helen Marsden/Getty, 18–19; Deborah Kolb/Shutterstock, 20–21; PAKULA PIOTR/Shutterstock, 22tl; O _ Schmidt/Shutterstock, 22bl; Rob Marmion/Shutterstock, 22tr; Inc/Shutterstock, 22br; Steven Frame/Shutterstock, 24.

Printed in the United States of America at Corporate Graphics in North Mankato, Minnesota.

Table of Contents

Working for Money 4

Ways to Earn Money 22

Picture Glossary 23

Index 24

To Learn More 24

Working for Money

We need money to buy things.

How do we get money?

We earn it.

How?

By working.

Max's mom has a job.
She grooms dogs.

She is paid after she grooms each dog.

Max's dad sells cars.

He makes money each time he sells one.

Ella's mom is a doctor.
She gets a paycheck.
She earns the same
pay each week.

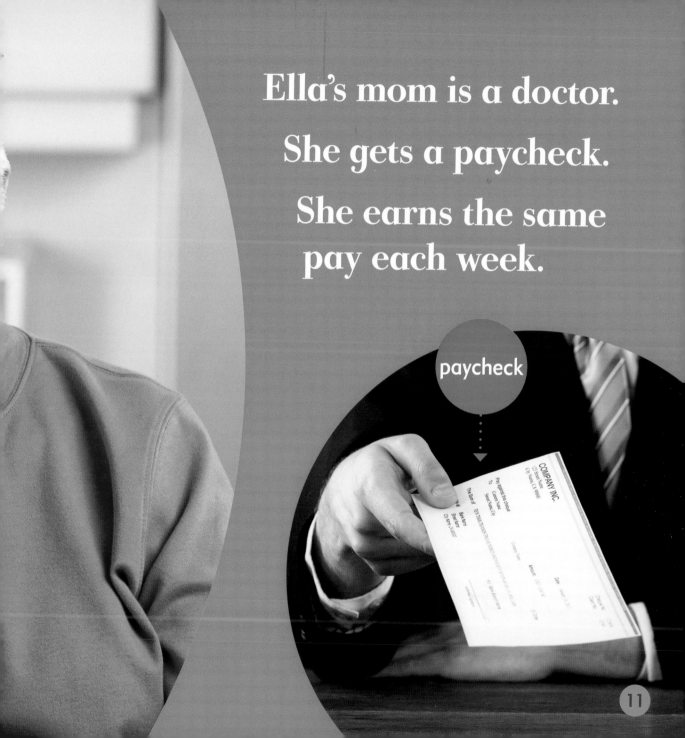

paycheck

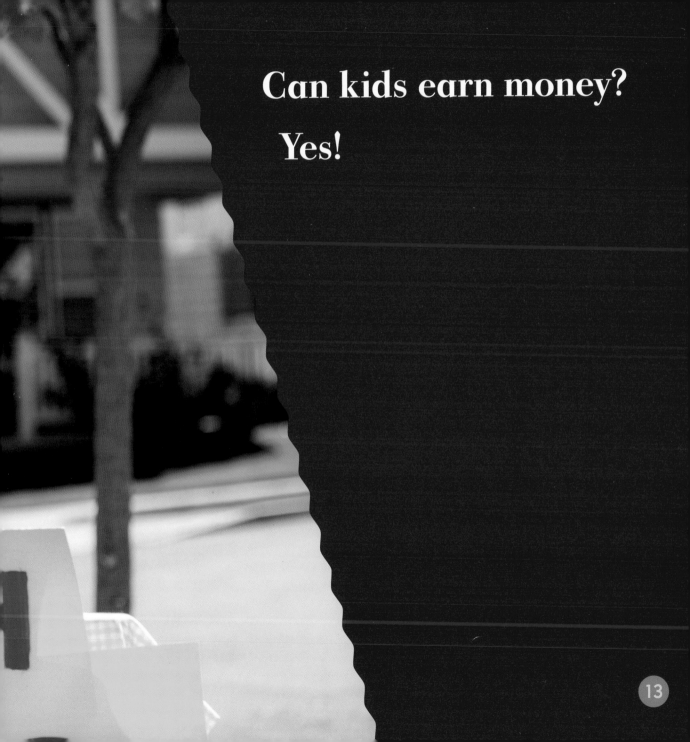

Can kids earn money?
Yes!

Max makes cards.

He will sell them.

Ella has chores.

She does extra
to earn money.

Sam waters his neighbor's garden.

He is paid each week.

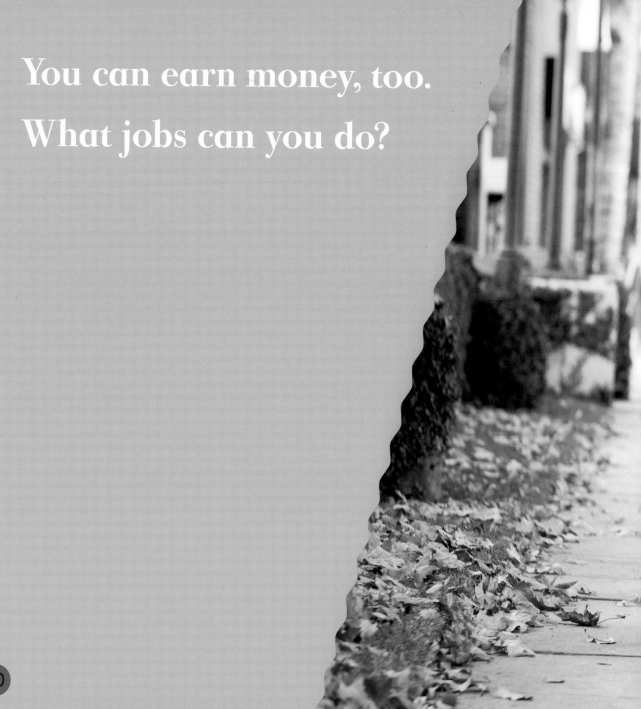

You can earn money, too.
What jobs can you do?

Ways to Earn Money

housework

selling lemonade

selling crafts

yard work

Picture Glossary

chores
Light jobs done around the home.

paycheck
A check earned for working.

grooms
Brushes, washes, and cleans.

sell
To give something in exchange for money.

Index

buy 4

cards 14

chores 16

earn 5, 11, 13, 17, 20

job 6, 20

kids 13

money 4, 8, 13, 17, 20

paid 7, 19

pay 11

paycheck 11

sells 8, 14

working 5

To Learn More

Learning more is as easy as 1, 2, 3.

1) Go to www.factsurfer.com

2) Enter "earningmoney" into the search box.

3) Click the "Surf" button to see a list of websites.

With factsurfer.com, finding more information is just a click away.